Risking
the
Wind

BOOKS BY WARREN CARRIER

NOVELS

The Hunt, New Directions, 1952
Bay of the Damned, John Day, 1957
Death of a Chancellor, Dodd, Mead, 1986
An Honorable Spy, Mayhaven Publishing, 1992
Murder at the Strawberry Festival, Mayhaven
   Publishing, 1993. *Justice at Christmas*, 1999, and
Death of a Poet, Denlinger's Publishers (Internet), **1999**

POETRY

The Cost of Love (chapbook), 1953
Toward Montebello, Harper & Row, 1966
Leave Your Sugar for the Cold Morning, St. Andrews
   Press, 1977
The Diver, QRL Poetry Series, Princeton, 1986
An Ordinary Man, QRL Poetry Series, Princeton, **1997**

TRANSLATION

City Stopped in Time, New Directions, 1949

EDITED

Reading Modern Poetry (with Paul Engle), Scott,
   Foresman, 1955
Guide to World Literature, editor, National Council of
Teachers of English, 1980
Literature from the World (with Bonnie Neumann),
Scribners, 1981

Risking the Wind

Warren Carrier

BIRCH BROOK PRESS

First edition
Library of Congress Catalogue Card No.: 99-96301
ISBN: 0-913559-56-3

Wood engravings by Frank C. Eckmair

Designed, typeset & printed letterpress at
       Birch Brook Press
       PO Box 81
       Delhi, NY 13753
Write for free catalogue of books & art.

Acknowledgments

The Ohio Review for "The Lady and the Fan," *Pembroke Magazine* for "Snow Geese," *Potpourri* for "Anniversary," *Visions-International* for "Jennifer Running," *Wallace Stevens Journal* for "The Hereness of Being," *Westview* for "The Dead."

for Tracy Marcia Elizabeth Joanna Rebecca
daughters of friends and friends

Men must endure
Their going hence,
even as their coming hither . . .
—Shakespeare, *King Lear*

Hence . . .

Going . . .

NOISE OF IMAGES

for Marcia

on the edge
the past in his mouth
brine
roses and slime

she rides in the cusp
like a knife
a sliding wall
collapsing
for miles

his guts unwind
blue and green
a rabbit stopped by shot
he forgets forever

THE SKATER

for Tracy

She skates the summer seawall,
unbroken miles of granite
and sand, conjugating
venir, aimer, voler
into a salted wind.
The earth draws her rolling
feet to its light
embrace; her head flies
like a seagull lifting
from a morning's catch.
The moon that pulled a tide
to the verge of rock
slackens beyond the steepening sun.
The skater soars, and we
are left with dazzled images
against the eye, suddenly here,
and suddenly gone.

NORTH OF NAPOLI

The birds diminish as they descend
to steps he climbs. They flurry up
to settle again when he has passed.
This is their fountain. Cracked cherubs
spout in the pool. The birds fluff
their wings in heaven's dirty water
and wait for crumbs from the empty *caffé*.
Steep walls of houses are wings for the square,
transporting it to a piazza of sky.
Black crepe pends from the great door
of a bleached palazzo. Beneath the crepe
angels and humans intertwine
in metal and wood, indifferent to the distant
squall of German guns. The crepe
is faded. The houses, abandoned, hang back
in the plash of cherubs pissing, the whish
of wings lifting as he descends.

SNOW GEESE
Wisconsin

He sees her face still as the seasons barter their edges,
and snow geese rise on great pommelling wings
from the Horicon marshes. Their grace loots the sky.
Their mournful cries ride all day on the wind.
Once fields flowed with light and the sun flamed forever.
Now, as time straitens, the horizon tilts slowly,
white as a feather, into untenanted darkness.
He carries her remembered cries as he follows.

THE HOUSE ON SIXTEENTH STREET

The dolls were burned.
She put them in a tree

where birds pick Indian bones.
They spoke in Spanish before the candle fire.

Smoke went through the roof
like a funeral pyre.

Suits were handed down to soot.
Pictures of old women

rose from the ashes.
The attic opens at the ends

to see the neighbors,
dolls, birds in a tree.

HORSE ON THE MOUNTAIN
Spain

A month of rain,
rainlogged hyacinths,
a gravity of green
in the olive groves,
grass gone loco . . .

Reading the poets,
plucking ballads,
dancing the *zarabanda*,
loving a green girl . . .

Ayyyy, let me gallop the wind,
ascend the mountain,
trade this sadness for the moon,
while Earth goes green
and crazy in the rain.

HE MUSES ON THE HERENESS OF BEING

He hums while he muses. His hum
is here. No one else in Texas

hears him hum. The sound of sea
breaking on the rocks below

is there. When the sea breaks on his hum
like horns and oboes on a solo singer,

it is here and there at once.
From his *Schlop* along the Rhine,

the Teuton theologian *spricht:*
being there is being, *dasein.*

But here is near, there is far.
Being is where we always are.

He hums along the Texas Gulf.
Above his hum the seagulls squawk

and plunge for food. Where they plunge
is their here when they are there.

But *being here* is not within their ken.
Musing about one's being here

is being here. His solo humming
is the music of his musing.

And here at the oyster bar, *die auster*
is the music of his musing's being.

THE FICUS TREE

He sits beside the ficus tree and eyes
a brouhaha of heaven beyond his pane.
The ficus leaves shine like silken lies
in their porcelain urn. The wind's complaint
is muzzled. The leaves hang true, unruffled, deft.
He reckons the intent of wind by pitching clouds.
He reckons his life by a ficus tree: a weft
of silk sleaving in his skull. Out
of glass, mounting squally nature, sky
is bent. He knows the true by knowing lies.

JENNIFER RUNNING

A slanted sky cambers down to dark.
Comets loop in ellipses, flare out of sight.
Leaves break south, flit like pipits on the quad.

Ecco lovely Jennifer, submerged
in moon, an invention of bosky earth itself,
running like a leaf, pitched to learn

her season, then to go in the wind like any
she flurries through, autumn's scarlet fractures.
Gravity barely holds her for her while.

MORNING
La Jolla

her first face
fashioned of mist
gliding
through eucalyptus trees

below
the sea westward
losing itself
in a thicket of clouds

drifting
into the scent of the trees
a body into mist
evanescent

pale windows
set for burning
starlings on the walk
waiting for sky

SHORE LINES

angled sun
sea surfaces
bleeding houses
longlegged nymphs
pink flamingos
lead sun
pale swimmers
rocks

DAYBREAK

A breeze off the water bends
the hibiscus almost to ground
and lofts the screeches of gulls
at the sun's bloody rift.

The windscape of the red hibiscus
punching into the aurora
and dancing, its genius
invisible, mimes

the enigma we now abjure:
our bodies' nocturnal motions,
almost conjoined,
their sources unseen.

Spent, abstracted,
with California oranges,
muffins and jam,
we watch the ballet of the red

hibiscus and listen to raucous
gulls beyond our ken,
tilting keenly above
their morning's innocent prey.

ANNIVERSARY
Galveston

The hurricane that blew off the roof
and fractured the fence
between us and our uppity neighbors
was omen enough.

The popcorn tree, the magnolia,
the squabby fig,
the pear trees, all survived.
New roof, new pergola,

and the neighbors moved away.
I never thought
we'd last those humid years,
disc decay,

slack cancer, breaking
waves, birds
that squeaked in the crooked palms,
angular rain.

Now the passage begins
one turn more:
we reckon the circular sky,
risk the wind.

SHOOTER

for Marilyn

In light on dark, in dark on light, you catch
the woodlike gnarls, the leather wearing brittle,
the ends of bones that snaggle gums: a face.
You filch her rotted breath away in a click.
A child looks out from ancient eyes: a mother,
a sister, daughter, kin, a sun-dried village
that stretches back, untold. Her spirit hovers
in dust and draws you into sorrowful myths.

In spectrum red you meet the forms that rise
miraculously from aught: a gentle shrew
ascendant from a dark of ravaged years.
And so is beauty wrested, summed, alive.
And so her singular anima appears
to fix in time. Your photograph is you.

THE FAMOUS POET

He ate his life and left himself behind,
crumbs, bottles, wives, bloody urine,
and lines and lines on CD roms and paper,
swaggering themes, unbuckled rhymes, contrived
to celebrate himself, his notorious capers.

Now we set a stone among its neighbors
where the last of him, at last suppressed, reclines.
In the light of nature's bounty, he died a pauper.
His organic, bloated self will feed the worms.
If they also eat his words, we will not mind.

THE KEY

Her hair leaks out from under her hat.
Her face is the color of oil.
The key that hangs in a noose from her neck
will open the door to secrets
you don't want to know.
Her arms splay wide to take you in.
The sky shuts down behind her.
Her key shines like the silver cross
you kissed before you died.

SHORT STORY

Edna, dreamer, poet, tree hugger, prodded
Charles to father a child in the image of the God
who, in his infinite whimsy, had given her both
a hump in her back and a liar's nose.
Spirit willing, but flesh quaggy, he was no match
for her love of villanelles and embraceable oaks.
Surely, God knows, he did not lack for ruth,
but nature, without desire, buckles the root.
A sailor got her with child and vanished in the War.
The child was healthy, forgiven. I know no more.

TRACY

She smiles among the paper buffaloes,
a little wild in a herd of art,
a piece of art, as much as humans are,
herself, free, but fencing as she goes

the self she gradually makes of what she is.
A continent away, beemen seek
wild honey in the giant trees.
They offer to their god a gift that's his.

This is your share, they say. This, our life.
Save us, please. And so we say: savor
this sweetness; it is yours. But keep her safe
in forests, on plains, against the beasty night.

THE LADY AND THE FAN

His mother's Japanese fans,
unfurled in a rosewood étagère,

show delicate trees sketched
with a single stroke of the brush.

She stands with the fan
she treasures most,

a kimonoed lady standing among trees
at the edge of a stream,

covering her face with a fan,
except for her eyes.

His mother is looking in the mirror
that hangs in the passageway,

holding the fan
that holds the lady

holding a fan.
It covers her face,

except for her eyes.
He walks along the sand.

Lights come on
in the windows of the beach houses.

Hence . . .

HARRY IS DEAD

It's strange, isn't it, Harry said. And died.
All his words unraveled in a trice.

The students sat in rows and waited.
Harry looked out the window.

Back in Minneapolis
there was no one left at the furniture store.

Books lingering to be read or written
lay neatly on the table top.

The news circulated slowly
in Cambridge and in Paris.

In the end he looked like Don Quixote.
What is there to say?

What he said himself.
Harry is strangely dead.

THE UNEXPECTED

Glittering crystals skimmed the roof.
Grass hunched low, rimed to the roots.

Portents. This was the way it would **come**:
a sudden cold, a heart gone wild,
a shivering in a forgetful sun,
southering birds floating high,
a skewing down till his voice fell dumb.

SEXTA HORA

He sits beneath the popcorn tree
wincing at pinched discs.

The muted swoosh of surf
rides an offshore breeze.

A siren yowls
far to near to far.

He broods and nods.
Birds that woke him

from fidgety dreams at dawn
will gorge the trees again

with their melodious
dissonance at dusk.

The moon will lift the sea
and smooth a tide to cluttered sand.

Sounds become distant,
the breeze declines.

He slumps to silence,
encumbered by persistent earth.

SING GODDAMN

The last hibiscus shudders in its bed
as skies fume south from dark refineries
to scatter hues in whits of flagrant red.
A winter night comes on. The last of leaves
are borne by skirls of wind along the eaves.
The birds ride squalls to islands in the gulf.
I learn my life from wind and scuffled leaves,
descending, drifting on a tilted globe.
Hibiscus, motlies, soot invest the air,
collect in corners of my mind like driven
debris. As shocks streak down my arms I flare
in words. I am a battened scrivener
of bits and pieces. When the final green
recedes, I scrawl them to a winter's genius.

AFTER ALL

Say what matters.
Don't drag us through the dust of old buildings again.
Say it in irony. And laugh.
We'll join you at the table
with champagne and lamb and pineapple cake
in the noise of our history,
in the tick of your honor.
After all, you don't have much time
before the party is over
and we scatter to the rest of our lives.

THE NAKED TREE

Here the naked tree,
the weathered boards of the fence,
the white chair
where he sat in summer
listening to the repetitions of birds . . .

The tree did its *danse macabre* in the wind.
The chair was abandoned to winter rains.
The sky went blind.

His memories flicker
in their habitual carousel.
He waits for the apposite moment,
for limbs to leap
in a final gambol
before their rooted sleep.

CIAO

A powder of bones lies in a white hot string.
Water becomes air.
A sooty tern slacks against the wind.
Light skates on the water.
Mountain shadows list
eastward from the scuttling sun.
No one notices your burning.

A DAY AT THE BEACH

We sat on sand with birds
in the lacy skirts of surf.
The day poured down.
Bach's three-part inventions
rose from a box.

Sea jockeys sat
on their boards like gulls
waiting for God.

A diver came up like a seal
with mother of pearl.

We watched and burned.
We listened to fictions of the dead
in luminous shells,
aluminum discs.

They muted at last
when there was no one in the thwart of the tide
to ride down a ridge
or put an ear to time.

POSTCARD

He gazed beyond the rocky edge where turning
maples stretched for miles, particulars
of his mind, a village, a white spire.
Above the turquoise atmosphere, an unseen
gravity held all light within itself,
burst like a melon, scattering galaxies.
He thought of the momentary hues of maples,
of human generations, the same, and never
the same, of randomness, of order as change.
The black that cracked into its separate stars,
bloomed from bent and distant light, had come
to this: himself here, agaze and musing,
maples the tint of the sun, a village of beings
unseen under leaves, their immaculate spire.

PRUDENCE

He knelt in a field of rain,
and crushed the rampant grass
to find your stone.
Here the smell of earth is strong.
He heard his captured breathing
above the rain,
a grosbeak in the distant trees.

Earth itself is made of rain and scree.
Against the sounds of water, birdsong,
your tremulous soprano rose from the loft.
You praised your God
and held the human in your horny hands.
Your earthly lord of oratory,
of nights of biased learning,

of primal hurt, of clotted heart,
lies beside you
in his earth-bound box,
waiting for his ghostly morning.
You loved and catered,
bore him a steadfast daughter,
and sons—one in your image,

one a renegade you loved no less,
survived a score of years beyond,
went quickly in your proper time.
In time the earth will burn to rock again,
cycles of human breath unwind.
He read your name and knew
the numbers of your life would be his own.

THESE ARE THE ONES WHO DID NOT DIE

These are the ones who did not die.
They remember that they did not die.
They had come at last to the farthest point.
The tiny bird did not bring hope.
The sky that turned blue between the clouds
did not bring hope. They waited to die.
And when they did not die they donned
new clothes and moved to another country.
Now they listen to the tiny bird
that sings in the tree outside their window.
They walk on the street and along the shore
and watch the waves coming in and dying
and coming in again. They imagine
that the sound of the waves is the sound of the dead
crying faintly against the sky.

THE FIRST TIME

It was not what he expected:
something let go on its own,
a brooding bird that vanished into leaves.
It happened before he knew the names of things.
He lay on his back and sank into the astonishing sky.

There were others, of course, at random,
though he might have thought they were intended.
Now, knowing their names, he lies on the hard earth
to watch the drifting cumuli,
the indigo buntings that flit into live oaks.

EAST OF HAMMOND

When Father raised a hand to strike my face,
Princess took it gently in her teeth.
Surprised, and not a little in disgrace,
Father waited till his hand was free
then kicked her in the ribs. I intervened
and took the cuff originally deserved
for sins now out of mind. As one, we keened,
Princess in my arms, my head awhirl.

Hours of the dark I hear her whine.
A stranger gave her poison. She raided cans.
To live your only nature is a crime
for beast or man. I buried her in sand.
On top I piled a cairn of random stones.
Exiled now, far from Father's home.

LEAVES

The leaves that tacked the autumn windflaws
all sun long have wrecked in rows
against a break of ivied stone.
He loiters there in dusk and smoke.

How many autumns blown to fire
or heaped to mulch a bed! Desire
fails so, smoldering in his eyes
or hoarded to decay. The sky's

decline, pungent nature burning,
asunder in gold and fallen to earth,
publish his season: Eros and end.
He will not stop this way again.

THE DEAD

The dead have a life.
They live where I live.
In my restless bed.
In my salt-pitted window that gives on the sea.
In the forms of my flesh.
In my choices.
In my invented stories.

My grandfather skins a squirrel.
My father shouts from his pulpit.
My mother cans peaches from Michigan.
I carry anger and love over my shoulder
like stones in a sea bag.
The dead arrive in the morning
with flotsam on a storm tide.
At night they fill my ears with sad songs.

I READ THE HOUR

A star slopes south as a mizzling wind
summons the certain cold. I read the hour
and acquiesce to its perfect changes.
Years recede to detritus: eighty
on a ball of corroded stone and water.
I scrabble in its circuits. Bruited pages
bleach to ether.

                       Yet what beauty rides
in the rare pitch of things! In ripened boscs,
in Bach, in Donne, in Van de Rohe, Matisse,
the cant of the sea, in dear and difficult lovers.
Let it tilt! I walk on a bias to the end.

AT SEA

Beyond the last island,
sea fastens to sky.

Adieux that flare in the eye

blink out like lights on a sinking shore.

The last gull slues
and slides back.

Clouds gather and spend,
green as the water.

Each wave is an image of the last,
rising and wracking.

I recur and decline,
in the seas's ennui.

LATE AFTERNOON

He walks in pain and sits with Bach:
Ich ruf' zu dir, Herr Jesu Christ.
He descends to the deep interiors of sound;
he is caught into the opulent purse
of an autumn hibiscus.

Beauty is intricate as a seed
that bursts, dazzles, and falls into scars
in arrays of fire and cocks of memory;
beauty is intricate as a baroque chorale,
cadent and unrelenting
as the thrust and surrender of the sea.

As dark ascends, he watches the suave terns
reconnoiter from their usual orbits.
As Earth slips along its breaks,
he probes for easeful sleep.

NIGHTY NIGHT

Sleep.
Lick your nerves.
Ride a horn
through moldering rain.
Your corked desires clabber.
Your soul hangs like a grackle
over sculch.
Where poles melt,
slats separate the light.
Disconnect.
Sleep is practice for dark.

DECEMBER

When snow birds walk on the pond
and the noes of childhood crawl like lichen
into the cracks of walls
his memories crimp like crocuses underground.
When the bones of the old ones arch in their boxes
like branches of vacant oaks
his words flock against fences with a season's debris.
When the road falls away into snow-layered pines
the imminent beckons.

ABOUT THE AUTHOR

Author of six collections of poetry, six novels, and four other books, Warren Carrier is a university chancellor emeritus from Wisconsin, living in Galveston, Texas, with his wife, an associate dean at the medical university there, and his younger son, a senior at St. John's College in Annapolis.

HOW THIS BOOK WAS MADE

RISKING THE WIND was typeset in 12 pt. Binny Old Style, named after Scotsman Archibald Binny, one of the earliest typefounders in America. Metal text type was cast on a Monotype system and worked by hand. Text was printed letterpress with a V-45 Miehle Vertical on 80 lb. Mohawk Vellum, Cream White. Cover was printed by hand with a Chandler & Price platen press on 80 lb. Superfine Eggshell. Wood engravings were cut as original art for this book by Frank C. Eckmair. Casting and printing were done at Birch Brook Press.